ENERGY...
WHAT IS IT?

COMMONLY ASKED QUESTIONS
About "Energy and how it works
Plus insights into energetic healing therapies,
WITH PRACTICAL ANSWERS

Written by
Simone Goldrick

Copyright © 2013 Simone Elizabeth Goldrick
All rights reserved.
ISBN-10: 0987465309
ISBN-13: 9780987465306
Simone Elizabeth Goldrick

Inner peace,
Joy,
Happiness and
Self respect
Cannot be granted by
Someone else
Happiness lies within.

Blackheath – in the front garden of a lovely holiday house that I stayed in with my family in 2012

CONTENTS

PREFACE vii
INTRODUCTION ix

CHAPTER ONE

Energy...what is it? 1

    CH'I...WHAT IS IT? 1
    ENERGY...WHAT IS POSITIVE AND NEGATIVE ENERGY? 5
    ESOTERICS...WHAT IS IT? 6
    FENG SHUI...WHAT IS IT? 7
    INTUITION...WHAT IS IT? 10
    METAPHYSICS...WHAT IS IT? 10
    POWER OF THOUGHT...WHAT IS IT? 13
    TELEPATHY...WHAT IS IT? 16

CHAPTER TWO

How The Subtle Energy Works In Your Body 19

    ASTRAL...WHAT IS IT? 19
    CHAKRA...WHAT IS IT? 20
    MEDITATION...WHAT IS IT? 21
    MERIDIANS...WHAT ARE THEY? 22
    PENDULUM...WHAT IS IT? 24
    TAI CHI...WHAT IS IT? 25
    VISUALISATION...WHAT IS IT? 26

CHAPTER THREE

Therapies to aid the body in energetic healing 27

    ACUPRESSURE...WHAT IS IT? 27
    AROMATHERAPY...WHAT IS IT? 27
    BOWEN THERAPY...WHAT IS IT? 28
    CST...WHAT IS IT? 28

COLOUR THERAPY...WHAT IS IT? 29
DOWSING...WHAT IS IT? 41
LAUGHTER THERAPY...WHAT IS IT? 45
KINESIOLOGY...WHAT IS IT? 45
RAINDROP THERAPY...WHAT IS IT? 46
ENERGY TIPS...HOW TO USE IT? 47

CHAPTER FOUR

JOY...HOW DO I FIND JOY IN MY LIFE? 49
MAGNETISM...WHAT IS IT? 50
About the Author *55*

PREFACE

The aim of this book is to inspire you to apply the key concepts of energy, esotericism and metaphysics in ways that will allow your life to flow smoother. Greater benefits will appear if you simultaneously develop the physical, mental and spiritual aspects of your life. It's all about balance. Apply the following principles wisely and with some humour.

Energy or chi will be discussed frequently in this book. It is discussed in depth in Chapter One "What is Energy Flow?", however, here is a brief overview:

Although we all have our own separate forms of energy/chi we are all linked together with everything around us, which intrinsically has an influence on our daily lives. It is important to remember that we are individuals, but not separate. We are like a wave reaching its peak; crashing and then returning to the ocean only to form a wave again.

The aim of my business, **"Transcend to Excellence"** is to help you develop an understanding of how we are harmoniously in accord with the universe and each other.

Everything has a "flow" like a river. When we are in harmony with nature we flow down the river and every aspect of our life is balanced. However, when we are out of step with the natural rhythms of the universe, our lives can be a constant struggle – just like rowing a boat upstream.

It's all about harmonizing yourself with the natural energy of nature and your home environment.

INTRODUCTION

Spirit is always present. Spirit surrounds us, soaks into us, and we radiate spirit in every moment. Our lack of inspiration is not the absence of spirit in our lives. It is a lack of awareness.

When you know you have a negative, limiting belief, you are free to examine it and discard it if you choose. No choice exists for unconscious beliefs or unexamined attitudes.

The awareness generated from this book will hopefully reduce or eliminate self-sabotage. As well as -

1. strengthen your will
2. lead to improved energy
3. help create financial stability
4. improve relationships and
5. strengthen health

With this awareness you are able to make empowering choices daily.

It is about taking the next step…from what you know – to what you do. The choices you make are based upon your experiences and beliefs. These inner beliefs shape your outer world. This book is designed to provide you with guidance and practical ideas to assist with personal, professional and spiritual growth.

Focusing upon living and reacting within the realities of relationships, career, health, your worth, will power, money, emotions, fears, compassion and healing.

This book ties in Chinese acupressure and meridians and feng shui principles through the house and garden and universal energy flows; including positive thought, healing powers, magnetism and food.

Gaining energy from the sun and energy fields surrounding us. Determine whether you have positive or negative energy created in the space that you spend most of your time.

CHAPTER ONE

Energy...what is it?

CH'I...WHAT IS IT?

Chi = ki (Japanese) = qi = prana (Indian) =..... **Energy**

We all have our own separate energy fields around us; humans, plants and animals. Some of us are high in energy, some are very low. Some are fast and haphazard, others are relaxed and peaceful. We all radiate either a positive or negative vibe, which can vary day to day depending on our emotions at the time.

Ch'i or qi (pronounced "chee" and henceforth spelled "chi") is the Chinese word used to describe "the natural energy of the Universe." New Agers often refer to this energy as subtle energy. Chi permeates all things, including the human body. One of the key concepts related to chi is the concept of harmony. Trouble, whether in the universe or in the body, is a function of disharmony, of things being out of balance and in need of restoration to equilibrium.

Man-made vs. natural ch'i

Consider the following two office types:

One has an indoor fountain, lots of plants,
Open fireplace and views across the countryside.

The other has air conditioning,
Synthetic carpet and an abundance of electrical equipment.

The natural energy of the first office space positively charges the workers and hence promotes a happier and more productive workplace. How do you feel at your workplace?

DOES THE CHI OF OTHER PEOPLE AND ANIMALS AROUND ME AFFECT MY ENERGY?

Indeed it does! Your chi or energy will start to resonate with the corresponding energy. Imagine a little rapid mouse was running around you. Your heart will beat rapidly. As opposed to a slow, cumbersome tortoise; your heartbeat would slow down.

What is predecessor chi?

Does the life of previous tenants and owners affect me?

The walls, the floors, the furniture, ornaments, plants and pets adsorb things that happen in buildings. Any strong emotions that occur leave an energetic imprint. Have you ever had an overwhelmingly warm feeling wash over you as you enter a happy family home? Or have you ever walked into a room after a quarrel and felt the tension? Energetic imprints get absorbed by you whenever you enter the room.

HOW CAN I CHANGE / ERASE THESE IMPRINTS?

Issues are permanently recorded until cleansed.

>Cleansing can occur in a variety of ways:
>Music (classical or instrumental)
>Physically cleaning, sweeping and mopping
>Crystal cleansing
>Laughter
>Vibrational: using a Tibetan chime or singing bowl
>Sunlight. Open the curtains, the blinds and windows.

And, most importantly, the **intention** to cleanse the space.

ENERGY...WHAT IS POSITIVE AND NEGATIVE ENERGY?

Positive energy is .....

- Speaking kind words
- Being happy
- Optimistic (in thought, speech and action)
- Having faith and
- And having hope

….. In other people as well as yourself.

Negative energy is .....

- Speaking unkindly
- being pessimistic (in thought, speech and action)
- not having hope
- not having faith

….. In themselves or other people.

WHY / HOW IS THIS CREATED?

The energy in a place is created through the occupants' thoughts, words and activities.

Overall maintenance and cleanliness will positively influence your life. Putting good vibes into your home puts good vibes into your life!

ESOTERICS...WHAT IS IT?

Esoterics is the study of the different subtle energy systems in the body; such as auras, chakras and meridians.

It is the belief of the unseen forces that make up our energetic system.

Esotericism signifies the holding of esoteric opinions or beliefs.

Many practitioners work with esoterics as a guide to helping their patients. Some practitioners such as:

- Acupuncturists,
- Vibrational masseurs
- Reiki masters
- Energy workers
- And Iridologists.

To name just a few.

Feng shui...what is it?

To live a healthy, happy life ideally one should harmonize themselves with the natural energy of your home and nature.

Feng shui incorporates many ideas. It originated over 4,000 years ago in China. It is concerned with maximizing positive energy and harmony in the home, feng shui looks at the positions of rooms in the home, furnishing arrangements and colours to use for decorating, all of which ensures success and well-being for its' occupants.

Feng Shui is harmonising physical, mental and spiritual methods of healing by addressing the following ideas in particular:

SPARE ROOMS - Can become stagnant and thus stagnates the corresponding area in your life. It is very important to regulate the energy in spare rooms by entering, opening a window or burning incense.

Keep it neat and clutter free.

CLUTTER - A collection of unused items that is simply untidy. What you don't use, someone else may be in need of. So sell it or give it away.

When is it clutter?

Items that are no longer in any use to you. It is clutter if you have not used it in 2 years and are not likely to use it in the next two years.

Before you let something new into your life you have to let something go.

When energy can't flow it stagnates. Clutter creates stagnation and makes everything grind to a halt. It can make you depressed and tired. If an area of your home is blocked and stagnant it has a corresponding effect on that part of your life; whether that be your finances or your physical wellbeing.

ENERGY BLOCKS
HOW DO I IMPROVE RELATIONS?

Place a vase of flowers or burn an incense candle in the relationship area of your house and dedicate it to the person who has the ill feelings. Plant aromatic shrubs in the relationship area of your yard – dedicating it to the person.

Visualising you with the wealth you desire (see Visualisation)

HOW DO I IMPROVE MY WEALTH?

Visualize, and inwardly feel yourself with the wealth you desire (see Visualisation)

Suggestions for outside Heavy stable items for stable income. Rotation object for continual income (eg. Clothes line or windmill). A pond with healthy fish in it, a clean pool, or a healthy fruit tree.

Suggestions for inside crystals, an aquarium, a piggy bank with money in it, a picture of sea yachts or any other wealthy scene.

Visualising yourself with the wealth you desire (see Visualisation)

Is it bad Feng Shui to have my toilet is in the wealth corner?

That's O.K, as long as it is kept clean, fresh, aerated and with the toilet lid closed and the door closed.

HOW DO I IMPROVE MY HEALTH?

Suggestions for outside a healthy vegetable garden.

Suggestions for inside Fresh flowers, an aquarium, fresh fruit, candles, healthy plants and pictures, clutter free.

How do I improve my families' health?

Choose wisely and eat healthily.

Place fresh flowers in the house and/or light a candle dedicating it to the ill person with the intention to improve health of that person.

Below is a rough guide of where each segment of your house/yard correspondingly relates to each segment of your life.

WEALTH	FAME	RELATIONSHIPS
FAMILY/HEALTH	TAI CHI/ CENTRE	CREATIVITY/ CHILDREN
INNER KNOWLEDGE/ INTUITION	CAREER	HELPFUL PEOPLE

FRONT DOOR/GATE THIS SIDE

INTUITION...WHAT IS IT?

Intuition is the way our body and higher intelligence talk to us in order to help us towards our destiny.

It is something that comes to your attention suddenly and informs you to contact a particular person or to put a particular action into place.

The more we become open to our intuition, the more we will experience it. Awareness is our first step towards intuition, and then our body will talk to us in a direct way.

If something feels right, it is right.

Inner self talk is a reasoning process where we throw questions at ourselves and engage in a dialogue.

What intuition tells us to do is not necessarily what is best in the short term, but in the long run it is always in our best interest.

Follow your intuition – it will lead you on the right path for you.

METAPHYSICS...WHAT IS IT?

Metaphysics is the philosophical study of energy and how to use it to heal. Metaphysics is a branch of philosophy concerned with explaining the fundamental nature of being and the world, although the term is not easily defined. Traditionally, metaphysics attempts to answer two basic questions in the broadest possible terms:

1. "What is there?"
2. "What is it like?"

A person who studies metaphysics is called a metaphysicist or a metaphysician. The metaphysician attempts to clarify the fundamental notions by which people understand the world, e.g., existence, objects and their properties, space and time, cause and effect, and possibility.

Blackheath

POWER OF THOUGHT... WHAT IS IT?

There is constant exchange of vibrations between you and your environment and people with whom you come in contact. All actions both positive and negative create vibrations in the ether. These vibrations also pass through your body.

When I shake hands with someone I give them magnetism and sometimes when I want to receive their vibration, I receive.

Let love and peace flow through you continuously, then wherever you go you will be a magnet. Even at a distance you can change an enemy. Just send your love and good thoughts. If someone makes them self your enemy, go on trying to be kind to that person. Be friendly from your heart, and do something by which he will know you want to be friendly. If that doesn't work just silently give love. Change will occur. Love is powerful. Never misuse the power of love, but continuously increase it to help others.

WHY DO WE FALL ILL?

I have no doubt that illness (in addition to external factors) is caused by internal stress derived from unresolved unhealthy feelings. There is nothing wrong with feeling hurt or angry. But once the feeling is acknowledged you must get rid of that negative feeling as fast and as efficient as possible. There are thousands of ways to turn negative feelings into healthy ones. Some of them are meditation, open communication – for most unhealthy feelings are usually from unresolved communications. All our feelings can be healthy if we apply ourselves to talking things out. Another way of staying healthy and positive is staying away from judgmental ideas. Criticizing others is only a reflection of our own insecurities.

Negative thoughts will create fear, while positive thoughts will provide encouragement. One simple way to understand such a powerful statement is that "energy is never created or lost, it is only transformed."

Manage the negative thing that happened; ask yourself questions – what is really happening to me? What is the positive lesson that I am supposed to get out of this? Is it keeping me away from my goals and visions? Decide to be in a good mood. Focus on something that you are looking forward to. Find a positive in every negative.

Enthusiasm energizes the words and thoughts we use. Being a truly positive emotion it is bound to affect our total wellbeing. We will stand up straight and walk with a spring in our step. Interacting more positively with others is extremely contagious.

Find a reason to be enthusiastic.

Below is a poem for food of thought:

> *All it takes is one "hello"*
>
> *I took the time to say hello to someone that I didn't know.*
> *To someone who was walking by, a look of sadness in her eyes.*
>
> *And when she smiled back to me I realized my little "gift"*
> *Had given both of us a lift!*

*You never know just whom you'll meet,
throughout your day on any street
People just like you and me with loneliness and
problems too.*

*Yet life is always better when we take the time to
be a friend to someone that we don't even know
and all it takes is one "hello".*
Anonymous

HOW CAN THE POWER OF YOUR MIND HELP YOU LOOSE WEIGHT?

The mind is stronger than the body, so your diet is less important than a strong and positive mind. Our mental state can alter the way we process food. Our metabolism appears to be directly connected to our mental state. The same food will be processed differently according to whether we feel good or depressed.

Instill the thought in your mind, "I am losing weight" hold tenaciously to that thought and it will happen the thought should be so strongly established in your mind that the whole body will work at throwing off the excess weight.

Until you can accomplish it by mind power alone losing weight is best done by combining mind power, visualization, and exercise with proper eating. Consulting advice from a nutritionist for the right combination of foods is advised.

By strengthening your thoughts you can reach whatever goal you want to attain.

Exercise- daily stretches and a walk; eat plenty of fruits, vegetables, and nuts, cut down on starchy foods and sweets. In the beginning you will have an urge for something sweet, but be strong – make up your mind that you are going to loose weight and then follow through with will power. Don't be tempted. When this is achieved, a weekly treat is acceptable to satisfy those cravings.

Think thin!!!!

By strengthening your thoughts you can reach whatever goal you want to attain.

TELEPATHY...WHAT IS IT?

Telepathy is universal energy connection. Have you ever been thinking of someone and then they ring you? Or have you ever thought something was going to happen and then it did? The sending and receiving of thought patterns generally occurs between people that know each other well – example; close family members or best friends. These can be healing or informative thoughts.

Telepathy also commonly occurs between pets and their owners.

We are all connected through the ether, when in tune with ourselves and in turn in tune with the universe we can use telepathy.

CHAPTER TWO

How The Subtle Energy Works In Your Body

ASTRAL...WHAT IS IT?

The astral body

Also known as the emotional body is the carrier of feelings, emotions and character traits. It occupies about the same space as the physical body. The more confident the person, the stronger and clearer the astral body will appear.

Every change in emotions is radiated out of the aura of the astral body. Even fleeting emotions. This takes place primarily through the charkas and a little through the pores. Thus the astral body consists of an incredible display of constantly changing colours, shining in all imaginable hues. Fear, anger, depression or worry will form dark clouds in the aura, whereas love, devotion and joy will create bright and transparent colours to glow.

Our astral body stores all our unresolved emotions, fears and lack of self-confidence. These transmit their vibration into the external world. These energy vibrations, which we send out, attract the same energy vibrations from our environment (mutual attraction comes into play) which means we are frequently confronted by the people and circumstances we are trying to avoid.

We need to resolve all unresolved fears, aggressions and other emotional problems in order to reach your conscious goal. If emotional problems are not resolved, they will continue to recur throughout successive incarnations, since the astral body survives physical death and joins the new physical body after reincarnation.

Once we have fully understood these matters, we will have no other choice than to stop seeing ourselves as "victims" and making others or circumstances responsible for our weaknesses and misery. This realization in itself is liberating, for we take control of our own lives and ourselves.

CHAKRA...WHAT IS IT?

These are also the coloured layers of the aura. The auric layers are "breathing" energies around the human being that correspond to living energy. By contrast there is energy comparable to rays of light, shining both into and out of centres in the body. These centres are known as chakras. The chakras are lens like structures that collect and strengthen the light that surrounds us. Whereas the layers of the aura that surround the body produce "container" energy, the chakras provide the "content" of the container. These two energies are complementary, and work together to create and maintain life. There are seven main energy centres in the human body. Each of these centres contains a universal spiritual life lesson that we learn over time. The chakras are vertically aligned, starting with the base of the spine, ascending up to the crown of the head. As each person "masters" each chakra (each chakra is on average a 7 year cycle), he gains power and self-awareness that become integrated into his spirit.

Our chakras radiate when we are in balance and live a happy, healthy lifestyle.

MEDITATION...WHAT IS IT?

Keeping the mind still from the constancy of passing thoughts, allowing yourself to be still, any thoughts that come into your head let them pass, don't focus on them. Meditation allows the ability to acknowledge emotions, memories etc without getting tangled up in it. Thus clarity appears.

Life is less stressful in the PRESENT. Live in the PRESENT, be thankful for the past.

WHY DO PEOPLE MEDIATE?

The PHYSICAL benefits:

Tingles, numbness, relaxed, slowed breathing, heart slowed, heavy, sinking, merging, loss of proprioception, noises, dropped blood pressure, higher immunity.

The PSYCHOLOGICAL benefits:

Stillness of thought, peace, emptiness, bliss, clarity of thought, control of choices, increased concentration, increased awareness, and appropriate detachment (if needed).

The SPIRITUAL benefits:

Unity, realization of life purpose, inspiration, web effect, and inspiration.

> *"Meditation is one of the few areas of human endeavour where, if you're trying, you're succeeding."*
>
> **Dalai Lama**

Exercise; stretch and tense and release over the whole body. Focus on one chakra at a time.

MERIDIANS...WHAT ARE THEY?

MERIDIANS ARE AN ENERGY FLOW THROUGH THE BODY

We have energy flow through our homes and similarly through our body. When our energy or chi flows freely, we are healthy. When there are blockages we are unwell or out of balance.

The following picture shows the meridian lines as they flow through the body over a 24 hour period. To help restore balance to your body you could imagine the energy flowing through each meridian (following the direction of the arrow), beginning with the "liver", and finishing with the "gall bladder".

When I take the time to do this it always brings me a sense of balance and good health.

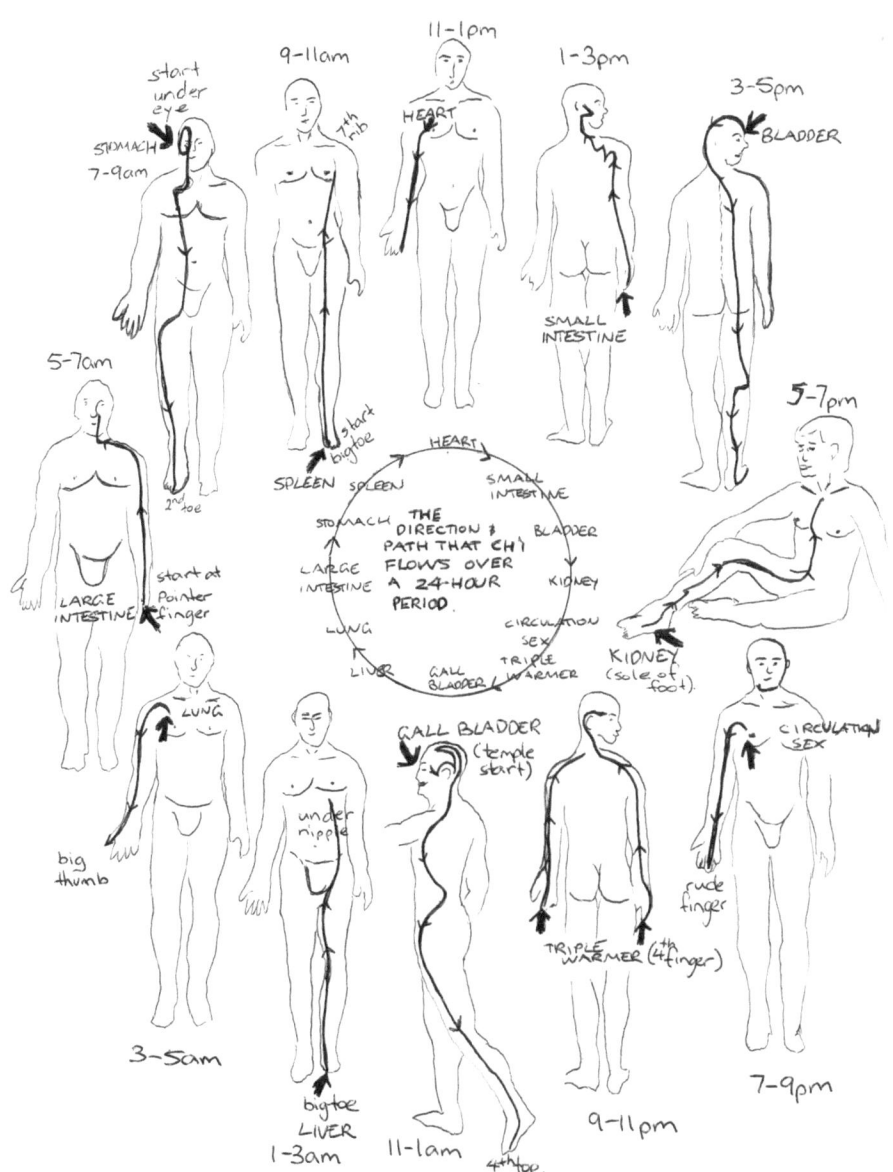

Meridians as they flow through the body over a 24 hour period.

Pendulum...What is it?

A pendulum is a tool used to tap into and sense your aura. It can be used to discover the truth of your state of well-being from your own energy field.

This tool helps to increase your sensitivities to the energy flow because it acts as an amplifier.

Preferably about one inch in diameter and one and a half inches long, it is pear shaped and symmetrical around its vertical axis (which is important for this type of measurement).

They can be made from pure crystal (which needs to be cleansed) or beechwood.

How do I know what it means for me?

Before you begin, make sure you are hydrated and calm. Then experiment with your pendulum; ask numerous simple questions that you already have definite answers to.

For instance, (for me) is my name Simone? The pendulum will move in a circular fashion – anticlockwise, clockwise or straight line. I have a definite yes. My "yes" is indicated by a clockwise motion, "no" is anticlockwise, and "maybe" is a straight line.

Experiment with your yes, no and maybe answers.

How do I diagnose my charka with a pendulum?

Lay on your back, hold the pendulum on a string about six inches long over a charka (eg the heart charka in your chest)

Empty your mind of all bias to the state of the charka.

Be sure that the pendulum is about two inches away from your body. Your energy flows into the field of the pendulum to energize it. This combined field of the pendulum and your energy then interact with the field of the subject, causing the pendulum to move.

The pendulum will move in a circular fashion – anticlockwise, clockwise or straight line. The size and direction of the pendulum indicates the amount and direction of energy flow through the chakra.

TAI CHI...WHAT IS IT?

Tai chi is a set of graceful, flowing exercises with a basis in martial arts. It is a moving form of meditation. With continued practice there will be improvement in posture and overall health. Among other advantages Tai chi helps develop self-control and concentration.

Visualisation...what is it?

"Whatever your mind can see and believe you can achieve."
Quote unknown

Your mind is a repository of infinite POWER.

So many people make themselves helpless by wrong habits.

Visualisation. Every day, upon waking and before you go to sleep, close your eyes and see yourself doing and being who you want to be. If you can, visualize with your eyes open during the day as well. Set yourself a goal and a realistic date by which you want it achieved – then strive for success.

ENERGY FLOW AND HEALING POWERS

Add an **affirmation** with your visualization.

One example may be:

"I am so happy and grateful now that I have the job that I have always wanted."

See yourself doing that job every day. Really live into and **believe** it!

CHAPTER THREE

Therapies to aid the body in energetic healing

ACUPRESSURE...WHAT IS IT?

Acupressure is an ancient form of healing. It involves the pressing of fingertips top key points on the surface of the skin to stimulate the body's natural ability to heal itself. Pressing on these points relieves muscle tension, which promotes the circulation of blood and qi (pronounced chee) – the vital energy or "life force" – to aid in the healing process.

AROMATHERAPY...WHAT IS IT?

Uses many essential oils derived from plant, herbs, flowers and roots. Aromatherapy involves the use of essential oils to elicit the desired effect; for example lavender is used to induce calmness and relaxation.

A few drops of an essential oil can be added to massage cream or oil and applied which enriches the massage experience and further aids the healing process, but it must be 100% therapeutic grade essential oil like that which we can purchase from Young Living essential oils. Other oils could be toxic to our health if they are not of therapeutic grade.

BOWEN THERAPY...WHAT IS IT?

Was developed by Thomas Bowen over 30 years ago. It is light touch and rolling strokes using the thumbs and fingers. This techniques works to manipulate the soft tissues to aid in circulation, lymph drainage and release energy blockages in the body.

CST...WHAT IS IT?

CranioSacral Therapy (CST)

Developed over 20 years ago by Dr John Upledger. Involves gentle head and neck massage which loosens restrictions and blockages that can contribute to pain and dysfunction; removing such blockages improves the functioning of the central nervous system and body as a whole.

CST is effective in treating a number of problems, including pain, headaches, central nervous system disorders, chronic fatigue syndrome, stress and tension. Proponents of CST also claim that it aids in improving mental clarity and emotional well-being.

COLOUR THERAPY...WHAT IS IT?
WHAT IS LIGHT COLOUR AND HOW DOES IT EFFECT ME?

The power of colour is a part of the natural energy of the universe. When we learn to see beyond the manifest physical world, we gain insight into the principles at work in the universe and begin to have a vision of the full beauty and inter-connectedness of everything around us. Patterns of energy interactions within and around the body are similar to those that occur around every living entity in nature. Although they are not normally visible to the human eye, they can be sensed or felt in other ways including the use of a pendulum. Illness develops out of imbalances of certain energies that may have occurred or been created at the emotional or spiritual levels, or that result from changes at a physical level. With this understanding the techniques of colour therapy can assist the body to heal itself. Colour practitioners can correct imbalances of energy inside the body using a variety of techniques that have been tried and tested over the last hundred years.

You can tune your senses to the vibrations of colour through dowsing. Record the results as you move down the chart, noting the strength of the response.

Dowsing like any other skill involves focus and practice. When people dowse, they use the ability of their bodies to feel and react to subtle energies, which cannot be detected by scientific instruments. Just as no scientific instrument can measure why people instinctively can feel danger or impending disaster, a dowsing pendulum can reflect a person's reaction to subtle energies.

RELATIONSHIP TO OWN CURRENT UNDERSTANDING, AND PRACTICE.

In many ancient cultures the sun was worshipped. The most important aim of life was for man to realize the light and thereby God. The effect of colour on life was of great significance to early human beings, whose very existence was governed by light and darkness. Most living things appear to be vitalized by the reds, oranges and yellows of daylight and calmed and rejuvenated by the blues, indigos and violets of the night.

Instinctively when I have a cold or flu I feel the need to sit in the sun and soak up the sun's rays. On doing this I feel the sun healing me through my eyes and face especially. During winter time when the sun is not there I feel a little low, especially when I am sick and there is no sun. Sometimes when I open my wardrobe I feel like wearing a particular colour that day, I find myself looking at the shopping centre for a pink or green top. This happens a lot. Colours affect the way I feel on a particular day.

When I meditate I imagine breathing in golden light to each of my chakras one at a time.

Using visualization and breathing techniques and affirmations all connected to these healing techniques.

When a drop of rain is drawn from the heavens, it is one of many. When it falls on its journey it changes shape constantly. But eventually when its journey ends it is as it started – a drop of water. Only the essence has changed through the many lessons learnt along the way. Remembering always that all the lessons we go through in life are temporary and delusive. As we pass a lesson so we progress to the next, each time progressing towards the ultimate – enlightenment.

Light is a narrow band of visible energy in the middle of a spectrum that embraces energies from cosmic rays to radio waves. These energies can be graded according to wavelength and measured in nanometres, each equivalent to one millionth of a millimetre. Each variation in wavelength within this band of energy can be sensed by our eyes and interpreted as a specific colour. Reds have the longest wavelength, lowest frequency and least energy, while violets have the shortest wavelength, highest frequencies and most energy. Colour breathing; breathing does more than bring oxygen into your blood and remove carbon dioxide from your blood. It sustains and revitalizes your spiritual energy. Concentrating on your breath also allows you to clear your mind of unwanted thoughts.

Breathe in orange for joy, happiness, and fun. Breathe out blue. Breathe in yellow to increase your objectivity and intellect. Breathe out violet. Breathe in blue for relaxation and peace. Breathe out orange. Breathe in violet to increase self respect, and for feeling of dignity and beauty. Breathe out yellow. Breathe in magenta to let go of any obsessional images, thoughts and reminiscences. Breathe out green.

In therapeutic touch, the healer must assess the patient's energies by passing her hands through the energy field surrounding the body two or three inches above its surface. Differences in energy flow resulting from imbalance are detected through sensations in the healer's hands, such as variations in temperature, pins and needles, tingling, pulsing, pressure or electric shock and associated colour imagery. The healer than relieves congestion by stroking or sweeping gestures away from the affected pat, and after washing or shaking her hands to remove the charge picked up from the patient, places her hands on either side of the affected area and imagines directing energy into it.

The techniques include the use of full-spectrum lamps, coloured crystals, silks and shapes; wearing coloured clothes, drinking solarized water, eating coloured foods, and the application of coloured oils during massage. In addition, the techniques of colour visualization, colour breathing and the use of movement enhance the effect of colour. The use of full-spectrum lamps in healing is probably the most powerful of the techniques available to the colour practitioner.

Our eyes are the most highly tuned of our organs for receiving coloured light. They supply about 90% of the sensory information available to the brain. However, information about light and colour also enters the body through the skin covering the whole surface of the body, even when clothed.

The most well known style of dowsing is with a water diviner, a forked stick that helps to concentrate the energies below ground level.

Using your finger, you can sense the amount and type of activity in the body, through the vertebrae. Once you begin working in this way you may find that it makes you more sensitive to working with colour in other ways too. Dowsing the spine requires you to firstly obtain a "witness" such as a lock of hair, a possession or a signature of the client and place it under the spine chart. Use the middle finger of your left hand, start at the top of spine. Let your finger hover about half an inch above the paper, move down the chart vertebrae by vertebrae, and allow yourself to feel the sensations. You will feel nothing over the inactive vertebrae. The active vertebrae will give you a hot, cold or tingling sensation.

HEALING WITH COLOUR

PHILOSOPHIES OF health and HEALING

Those who have never been deprived of colour tend to take it for granted, and generally don't realize its importance to our health and well being. Nevertheless it is a basic need.

According to ancient wisdom, energy in the form of light is drawn into the body's immaterial counterpart, which acts as a prism, breaking it down into seven streams corresponding with the frequency bands of the colour spectrum. Each of these is drawn through resonance to a chakra whose vibrations are of the same frequency. These vibrations become progressively more dense, heavy and lower in frequency along the vertical axis of the body. At its base they merge with and arise from the earth energies, represented in Indian thought as a coiled serpent – kundalini – and in Chinese thought by a dragon. The chakras, which may be thought of as transmitters or transformers of energy are believed to vibrate at a characteristic frequency as they distribute energy throughout the body. The energy patterns around each chakra, although always changing, are mostly of a certain colour whose vibrations correspond with its basic frequency. The prevailing colour of a chakra indicates how well its energies are being transformed and transmitted at a given time and therefore reflect current experience. Healing with colour is based upon understanding these principles.

The general principles followed by colour therapists are that energies can be stimulated by encouraging everyday exposure to certain colours. This can be through clothes and accessories or in the decoration and furnishing of your living and working environments, and by eating certain foods. The principal of resonance is used to determine which energies are expressed most by an individual. A person who usually wears a lot of red is assumed to be resonating with that vibration, and so may benefit from adding calmer colours of green or blue, if she tends to become "overheated" or excited or suffer from ailments associated with heat. By contrast, someone who suffers from not having enough of this energy and avoids wearing the colour may benefit from being surrounded by the colour. Such a person may also benefit from eating red food. Those who have an excess of red energy should avoid red food.

MODES OF HEALING

Coloured light can be projected on to parts of the body using various devices, including lamps and filters. Contemporary colour therapists use full-spectrum lamps fitted with special quartz filters that can produce colours of all wavelengths and frequencies. This cannot be achieved with ordinary artificial lights, because they emit some wavelengths more powerful than others. The spectrum of light emitted from a fluorescent tube for example is weaker in reds than blue, green and ultraviolet.

Forming images in the mind's eye, or visualization, is widely used in healing with colour. By imagining colour you produce vibrations of a certain frequency, which when directed to the energy centres of the body can produce various psychological and physical effects. In traditional Indian and Chinese medicine, visualising light being drawn into the body in various ways is recommended for self-healing. A common breathing exercise is to imagine breathing in coloured light. This is also practiced in many other traditions, ancient and modern.

Visualizing different colours into the body for different purposes, a couple of examples may be; red for vitality and increased sexuality, strength, and will power. Breathe out the opposing colour - turquoise. Breathe in green to cleanse, to feel more balanced. Breathe out magenta.

In therapeutic touch, the energy is modulated through use of colour imagery, so the healer mentally pictures sending blue energy to cool or sedate, red to warm or stimulate, yellow to energize, and continues to do so until the patient's body feels balanced.

Colour can affect our mood.

Each colour can have different affects for differing people, the following can be used as a general guide.i encourage you to experiement ….sit alone with a colour in mind and *feel* what that colour means for you.

RED

Can represent the following:

Fire, hot colour and therefore stimulating

Strength, vigiur, happiness, warmth, good luck and sensuality

Helps overcome sadness and depression

Good colour for people requiring high energy levels

Too stimulating for the bedroom

If used in the dining room people tend to drink too much and guests will tend not to go home

Restaurants use this colour to increase the sale of alcoholic beverages

In a bathroom red can be used to ensure that certain members of a family do not stay in there longer than they should.

Painting your front door or letterbox red will direct the chi and ensure that people know where you are

In children's bedrooms can be overstimulating and add to hyperactivity

A red ribbon can be fixed under the marital bed to symbolise holding the marriage together

Painting a handrail (or the underside) to a staircase red will help to take the energy upwards

Anthroposophy sheds another light on red. When we see red we also see green (the opposite on the colour wheel).

PINK

Can represent:

love, relationships, femininity, joy, nurturing, romance, happiness

Pink bedsheets will improve a relationship

Rose-quartz crystal generates pink, feminine nurturing energy

Pink is healing and soothing as it raises our vibration so it is a very healthy colour to have around you.

ORANGE

Can represent:

happiness, optimism and being sociable

Spirituality

Anthroposophy sheds another light on orange. When we see orange we also see blue (the opposite on the colour wheel).

BROWN

Can represent:

Stability

Dullness

A settling and earthy colour

YELLOW

Can represent:

Sunshine, gold, tolerance, patience, wisdom, happiness, optimism. Personal power and self worth.

The element of earth, particularly the ochre tones

Good for offices of sales people

A world –famous food outlet uses yellow to associate its product with happiness, but also to encourage their patrons to eat quickly and leave.

Good for children's bedroom to get them up in the morning, not good for relationship in parents room = chastity

Not good in kitchen – people will congregate there but not stay to wash up.

Good for study and concentration.

Anthroposophy sheds another light on yellow. When we see yellow we also see purple (the opposite on the colour wheel).

GREEN

Can represent nature, soothing, health, balance, harmony, rest and abundance

A healing colour

Good for waiting rooms

The element of wood, season of Spring

Anthroposophy sheds another light on green. When we see green we also see red (the opposite on the colour wheel).

BLUE

Can represent Inner truth, inner peace, inspiration, contentment, faith, devotion and composure

Water, it is a cooling colour. Good for rooms that get too hot – such as rooms facing west.

The element of wood, the season of Spring

Light blue gives a clean fresh feel due to association with water and air.

Good in dining room for people who suffer from indigestion and heart burn

Anthroposophy sheds another light on blue. When we see blue we also see orange (the opposite on the colour wheel).

PURPLE

Can represent nobility, power, respect, good fortune, psychic awareness and trust in the future

Purple is a good colour for meditation and healing.

Anthroposophy sheds another light on purple. When we see purple we also see yellow (the opposite on the colour wheel).

WHITE

Can represent a combination of all colours

Purity, cleanliness, high spirituality, creative imagination and humility

The element of metal and the season of Autumn.

Can be sterile and cold, therefore a tint is usually recommended

BLACK

Can represent total absence of colour

Silence, deep water, contemplation, night, depression and dormant energy

Element of water, the season of Winter.

GREY

Can represent neutraityl, some perceive it as balance since it is black and white in harmony

Reduces productivity and makes people sleepy

It can be associated with winter coming and time for hibernation.

> ***Experiment for yourself to find out how you feel when you wear a particular colour.***

The primary colours – red, yellow and blue with the secondary colours (orange, green and purple) in between them.

Dowsing...What Is It?
PENDULUM DOWSING

Dowsing is an age-old technique for detecting subtle energies. The amount and direction of the energy flowing through a chakra can be detected using a pendulum. After a few seconds the pendulum will usually begin to move. Its movements may be circular, elliptical or from side to side; and smooth or erratic. The direction and radius of the movement show the amount and direction of the energy flowing through the chakra. The radius of the movement is related both to the strength and quantity of the energy flowing through the chakra and the energy of the dowser. The wider the radius the greater the energy flow. The speed of the movement indicates the rate of energy flow through the chakra. Very fast movement suggests that the chakra is being overworked, whereas a slow speed means that the energy flow through the chakra is sluggish.

Clockwise movement of the pendulum indicates an open chakra that is functioning effectively; the feelings and processes governed by it are therefore balanced and healthy. Counterclockwise movement indicates that the chakra is closed or blocked so that energy cannot flow through it. The result is that the feelings and functions governed by it are not balanced and are probably experienced negatively by the person. Between these two extremes the pendulum may describe various other movements. An elliptical swing indicates a left/right imbalance of the energy flow, and that one side of the body is stronger than the other. A severe right /left split is suggested by a back and forth movement of the pendulum at a 45-degree angle to the vertical axis of the body; the larger the pendulum movement the greater the amount of energy contained in the distortion. Back and forth movements of the pendulum parallel to the body's vertical axis or perpendicular to it also indicate energy distortion. In the former the energy is being diverted upwards and in the later downwards, suggesting that it is expressed inappropriately through a higher chakra, or suppressed. Chaotic movement suggests that there is considerable flux in the chakra and in its functioning. When the pendulum exhibits no movement at all the chakra is no longer functioning and is not metabolising energy from the universal energy field. This is an unhealthy state and if maintained over time, the person will become ill.

MODES OF HEALING

Pendulum dowsing consists of holding a piece of string with a solid object suspended at the other end. You can make your own pendulum using string, cotton, fishing line or wool with an object like a gold or silver dress ring or a key. Whatever pendulum you use make sure you choose one that feels comfortable to hold.

Once you have a pendulum, go and sit in a quiet spot without interruption. Pick up the pendulum string and let the pendulum hang vertically about two inches above your knees. Keep your hand very still. Then ask "is my name (Simone)?" before the pendulum stops ask, "Is my name (George)?" Do this several times daily, until you are confident about what every movement means. For some people the pendulum will move the first time. For others it may take practice over time. The type of movements people get will vary. Some will get a clockwise movement for 'yes' and anticlockwise for 'no', others may get a vertical or horizontal movement, or some other combination of these directions.

Generally the direction of response you get initially will always be the same, however, it is good practice to always check what is your 'yes' and 'no' on any particular day. Another good habit is to ask "is now the right time to dowse?" Every so often you may be too tired or not able to dowse for some unknown reason, and you are better waiting for another time if you get a 'no' response.

One way to start your practice is with simple questions with answers you know and keep the dowsing sessions to less than 15 minutes each day until you get used to the process.

Pendulum dowsing can be used to get 'yes/no' type answers to various questions for natural earth energies. For example, to find out how many underground water lines you need to correct to bring a place into balance, or the length or number of pipes to correct a geological fault or any one of numerous questions that need to be answered.

Pendulum dowsing can also be used to work out what vitamins you need. **Simply by asking yes/no answers**. In phrasing questions it is better to ask questions from your perspective, not that of your brother or friend. For example you might ask "from my perspective should a feng shui correction be applied here?" Should it be a mirror or a crystal or a picture or a plant? By using these words the feng shui correction should suit your needs.

Blackheath rainforest

LAUGHTER THERAPY... WHAT IS IT?

Laughter raises your vibration!

The physiology of laughter will take over the centre of your being. Like enthusiasm, laughter will set positive conditions for your mind to take action. It is a very effective way to cut down on our stress levels as our inner world gets rushes of positive chemicals, which in turn foster optimum conditions for biological and mental activity. If depression and sadness can lower the capacity of the immune system, imagine what laughter and happiness can do!

KINESIOLOGY...WHAT IS IT?

Also known as Touch For Health, Kinesiology involves the practitioner tapping into the clients energy system to obtain information in regards to patient allergies and/or food intolerances.

It is pain free, not invasive and very effective!

All the knowledge that we need to maintain our own personal health and well-being is stored in our own individual energy system. Kinesiology is a tool used to tap into that energy system to get the answers.

Raindrop therapy... what is it?

Raindrop therapy is the application of drops of essential oils to your spine to help aid the body in healing.

Different 100% therapeutic essential oils from *Young Living* are applied, appropriate to the individual's healing.

Energy Tips...How to use it?

- Open your perception, find your guidance and realize why you are here.

- We are discovering again that we live in a world full of sudden coincidences and synchronistic encounters that seem destined.

- Controllers make you feel weak – you can't think properly because they take your energy.

- When you need someone, help will arrive.

- Giving is the secret to keeping connected.

- Energy amplifies back and forth if we all do this humanity will take another step in evolution.

- Follow own intuition, not let others tell you what to do.

- Little daydreams we have may be seen as guidance.

- When we give to someone who is also giving we build energy among ourselves.

- Coincidences happen more the more you realize them and give thanks.

CHAPTER FOUR

JOY...HOW DO I FIND JOY IN MY LIFE?

Even if you were to satisfy every material desire you craved for. I want that car, I need to buy that house, that dress etc. the craving is only temporary. Before too long you become dissatisfied and tire of this item; want to improve it or simply crave for something else you need.

So do not seek fulfillment through material things or desires. Seek the unconditioned, indestructible pure bliss within yourself, and you will have found the ever existing, ever-conscious, ever-new joy. Unlike material pleasures, this joy is self- born, your self-expressing quality of spirit. Seek it and be comforted forever.

You are the one who is in control of your behaviour. You make your self-miserable or content accordingly.

Do not leave anybody out of your love. Keep everyone in your heart, and they will keep you in theirs.

In giving love, you will find love. Be open to other people's thoughts; their ideas and their beliefs. Keep an open mind, respect them and they will respect you.

When there is an equal balance between giving and receiving you will feel at peace.

There is Chinese proverb that says a good teacher is someone that always learns more than his students. Similarly you will learn more about yourself when you try to make a difference to others.

Simply by putting a "smile on your dial" can change your state of mind immediately. Stand up straight, chest out, shoulders back, put a grin on your face and your physical and mental well-being will follow. It is impossible to feel sad at that moment. Feelings can be developed.

Magnetism...What Is It?

MAGNETISM: THE INHERENT POWER OF THE SOUL

Why is it that when some people speak, everyone is enthralled, while others can say the same thing and no one is interested?

Magnetism. It is the power of the soul to attract or create whatever it needs for all round happiness and well-being.

People who are inwardly happy and at peace with themselves send positive, high vibrations and frequencies out into the universal atmosphere and attract the attention of others.

What effects magnetism? How can I improve / increase my magnetism?

Both the kind and the quantity of foods you eat effect your magnetism. Those who overload their system with meat, for example, diminish their magnetism. On the other hand, pure foods such as fresh fruit, increase magnetism. As to the quantity of food ingested, it should be just enough so that when you leave the table you are still a little hungry. Overloading the stomach drains the inner life force and causes a loss of magnetism.

DIET AND MAGNETISM

The Spleen/stomach meridian is the meridian line running down the top of the legs. Sitting in kneeling position opens up the stomach meridian and is therefore the ideal position to sit while eating. If this is not physically possible, sitting with a straight back also allows easier digestion as the stomach is not squashed. Having an open meridian = easier digestion. Sitting with a straight back = easier digestion.. Junk food takes energy from the body to process. However, Vegetables / fruit provide uplifting energy.

Energy is mainly in the stomach meridian between 5 and 7am, this is the major elimination time and is therefore an ideal time to eat breakfast.

Do not over eat – over eating stretches the tummy and makes you feel "full" and lethargic. Stop eating just before you are full. You will feel better and put less stress on your liver.

Don't be a diet fanatic

Balance your diet, and then forget it. Once in a while it is good to break your diet. Just don't make a practise of it and thus let it become a habit. Your body should be your servant, don't allow yourself to become its slave. Think of the power of your mind, believe and know that it is the repairer of your body. Live by that mind power.

Visualization – picture yourself with the figure you want to achieve and go about the means through correct diet and exercise.

How do you think a cow remains strong and healthy by eating only grass? Out of that simple food it gets all the elements it needs. Of course there are good elements in the grass to begin with, but the main thing is that the mind of the cow has been conditioned to believe that all it needs is grass, and its body responds accordingly.

When the body comes under your control, it will obey whatever you tell it through the powerful suggestion of your mind.

Drinking plenty of water keeps the body free from disease – but not with meals. Take a glass of milk in between meals it will help to keep the body healthy because milk supplies your body with all the elements that are necessary. But avoid cream in it – take skim milk, rice milk or soymilk.

When you are hungry for a snack the best thing to eat is fruit or a raw vegetable juice. Eat a hearty breakfast, a moderate lunch and a small dinner; as the energy is in your stomach and digestive system in the mornings.

My message to you is to regulate your body weight at will. Obey the laws of right diet. In general, follow a moderate diet that contains all the body requires, and eat only as much as the body actually needs. That is the way to stabilize the weight by proper eating. Listen to your body stop when you are full, you don't have to eat everything that is on your plate, save it for a snack later. Weight 5 minutes before you go back for seconds and dessert – are you really still hungry?

How can time be used more wisely?

Don't be a chatterbox - Idle talk dissipates your magnetism. It is also dangerous, because if you talk too much you may say something harmful. Words have the power to explode empires or to bring peace. You can change others with your words. That is magnetism. Therefore, think before you speak. There is an old Taoist philosophy that says "Empty heads have long tongues". Some may interpret this to mean that the person who talks too much is a shallow thinker and thus has little magnetism. However, this is not always the case.

Watch your thoughts. All your experiences come through your thoughts. It is the company of your thoughts that uplifts or degrades you.

Try each day to do something worthwhile, so you feel you have made a contribution, that your life has some meaning. This will create great magnetism.

Bibliography

Birbsall, G. (1998) Feng Sui. The ancient art of placement.
Australia: Waterwood Management Proprietary Limited.

Graham, H (1996) Healing with Colour
Australia; Millennium Books.

Gunstone, J and Pascale, O. (1994) COLOUR THERAPY how to use colour to enhance your life, health and well-being..
Australia; Viking Penguin Books.

Myss, Caroline (1996) Anatomy of the Spirit
Bantam Books

Simpson, Liz (1997) The Book of CRYSTAL HEALING
Australia; Simon and Schuster.

The Cooranbong Gazette- Alan Butt (massage therapist)
The Celestine prophesy - movie

About the Author

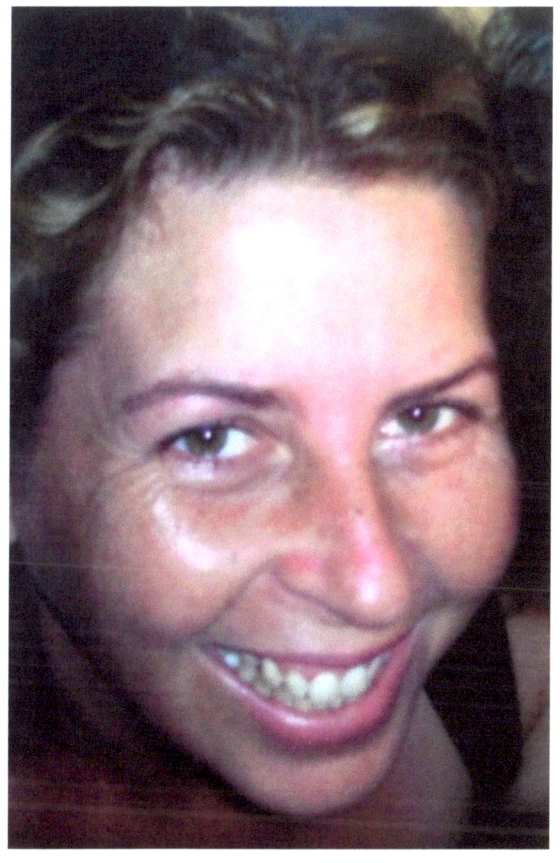

Simone Goldrick is a qualified teacher, she has a Bachelor in Education and a Diploma in Teaching. After many years teaching main stream, Simone is currently a Waldorf Steiner kindergarten teacher.

Simone Goldrick has studied Energetic and Spiritual healing through a number of different avenues, one of which was the Diploma in Energetic and Spiritual Healing including study of the subtle energy streams, Holistic Counseling and Feng Shui among many more.

Simone has a Catholic and an Anthroposophical background and has researched and experienced a variety studies. Simone has been on a self- realization journey beginning with Intense Informal study, since fourteen years of age, of Chinese medicine; including hypnotherapy, acupressure, herbs, energizing exercises, tai chi, martial arts and visualizations and aromatherapy.

Simone has dabbled in dance choreography and, for many years, Kung Fu instructing and training. And then further self-realization from her Indian philosophical study of Paramahansa Yogananda's teachings.

All of which fall under the umbrella of her.business: "Transcend to Excellence - set yourself free" by enhancing your whole self; body, mind and spirit.

Enhance your body with exercise and fitness;

Enhance your mind through education, study and research

And, enhance your spirit through personal growth and reflection.

Simone is on an Anthroposophical journey and is an applicator of bio dynamics and bio agriculture.

www.ingramcontent.com/pod-product-compliance
Lightning Source LLC
Chambersburg PA
CBHW041642090426
42736CB00034BA/7